THE ANAYA **SUN SIGN** *COMPANIONS*

GEMINI

22 May-22 June

CELESTINE O'RYAN

ANAYA PUBLISHERS LIMITED
LONDON

First published in Great Britain in 1991 by
Anaya Publishers Ltd., Strode House, 44-50 Osnaburgh Street, London NW1 3ND

Copyright © Anaya Publishers Ltd 1991

ASTROLOGICAL CONSULTANT Jan Kurrels

Managing Editor	Judy Martin
Art Director	Nigel Osborne
Designers	Sally Stockwell
	Anne Clue
Illustrators	Marion Appleton
	David Ashby
	Lorraine Harrison
	Tony Masero
Indexer	Peter Barber

British Library Cataloguing in Publication Data
O'Ryan, Celestine
    Gemini. – (Anaya sun sign companions).
    1. Astrology
    I. Title
    133.52
    ISBN 1-85470-092-8

TYPESET IN GREAT BRITAIN BY MIDFORD TYPESETTING LTD, LONDON
COLOUR ORIGINATION IN SINGAPORE BY COLUMBIA OFFSET LTD
PRINTED IN SINGAPORE BY TIMES OFFSET LTD

CONTENTS

GEMINI

*Most people know their own sun sign, and you know
that yours is Gemini, but do you appreciate its full
impact on every area of your life? Your* Sun Sign
Companion *is a guide to the many pleasures
and preferences that are specific to you as a
Geminian subject.*

*Your personality profile is here – and much more. You
can find out not only where you fit into the grand
astrological scheme and the ways the other zodiac signs
connect with your own, but also discover the delights of
the Geminian foods that are your special delicacies; the
plants that you should grow in your garden to enhance
your Geminian moods; the animals that you
appreciate for their affinities to your sign and the pets
that you as a Geminian can easily love and live with;
the ways in which you need to take care of your body,
and how your health and well-being may be affected
by the fact that you were born under Gemini.*

The fascinating range of this Sun Sign Companion *explains your temperament, your actions and the ways you live your life in zodiacal terms. You are active and adaptable and your special element – Geminian air – makes you communicative and quick-witted; your planetary ruler Mercury, the messenger of the gods, encourages your versatility. You have singular connections with the powers of the Earth itself – its gemstones, metals and crystals. And your zodiacal profile is underlined by your Geminian connections to the ancient and mysterious arts of the Runes and the Tarot.*
This book provides you with the intriguing mosaic of influences, interests and attributes that build into the total picture of yourself as a Geminian. More than any other zodiacal guide, your Sun Sign Companion *reveals to you the inherent fun and enjoyment of life under Gemini.*

THE ZODIAC

When the ancient astrologers studied the sky at night, they tracked the obvious motion and changing shape of the Moon, but noted two other phenomena: the frosty grandeur of the fixed stars and the different movements of the five observable planets. Mercury, Venus, Mars, Jupiter and Saturn moved and weaved about the night sky in repeating patterns, always within the same narrow strip of the heavens. And in the day time, the Sun could be seen progressing along the centre of this strip on its apparent orbit. Most of the action, celestially speaking, appeared to take place in a restricted

heavenly corridor. Astronomers and astrologers therefore gave priority to this ribbon of sky, and noted what else appeared in it.

Sharing the strip were twelve fixed star constellations, known from ancient times. They were Aries the Ram, Taurus the Bull, Gemini the Twins, Cancer the Crab, Leo the Lion, Virgo the Virgin, Libra the Balance, Scorpius the Scorpion, Sagittarius the Archer, Capricornus the Goat, Aquarius the Water Carrier and Pisces the Fishes. As most of the constellations are named after sentient creatures, the Greeks called this band of sky the zodiac, from their word meaning images of animals or living beings.

In astronomical terms, the constellations take up varying amounts of sky and exhibit different degrees of brightness. Astrologically, they are assigned equal prominence and importance, and are given equal 30-degree arcs of the celestial band. These are the signs of the zodiac, and the starting point on the celestial circle is 0 degrees Aries, which was the point of the vernal equinox over 4000 years ago when the zodiac was established.

The celestial jostling along the zodiacal corridor is explained by the fact that the planets orbit the Sun roughly in the same plane. Imagine yourself at the centre of a race track, timing a group of runners as they lap the circuit, each one running at a different pace and in a different lane. Soon you would be able to predict when each one would pass you, especially if you noted down landmarks along the spectator stands behind the runners.

In the same way, astrologers pinpoint the position and motion of any planet, using the zodiac band as a reference grid. Interpretation of the effects of planetary power filtered through the zodiac grid is the enduring fascination of astrology. The planets are extremely powerful, as signified by their having been awarded the names and attributes of the gods.

ZODIACAL INFLUENCES

 our sun sign is the zodiac sign that the Sun, the most powerful of the heavenly bodies, appears to be passing through from our viewpoint on Earth at the time of your birth. It takes the Sun one year to progress through all the signs, and it is the Sun's huge power, filtered through each sign in turn, that etches the broad character templates of each sign. Over the centuries, each sign has acquired its own repertory of characteristics and personality traits, a seamless blend of archetypal myth and particular observation. So now we can talk about, say, a 'typical Gemini' with the expectation that others will know what we mean. However, fine tuning and modification of the individual personality are dictated by two conditions at the time of birth – the positions of the Moon and planets in the zodiac and the nature of the ascendant, the sign rising on the eastern horizon at the moment of birth.

The Earth spins counter-clockwise daily on its axis, but to us it appears that the Sun, stars and planets wheel overhead from east to west. Within this framework, the zodiac passing overhead carries with it one sign every two hours; therefore the degree of the ascendant changes likewise, which explains why two people born on the same day can have such varying personalities. The influence of the ascending sign, and any planet positioned in it, has a strong bearing on the formation of the personality. A Geminian with Pisces in the ascendant is quite a different kettle of fish to one with Capricorn ascending.

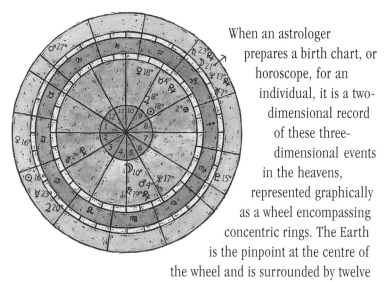

When an astrologer prepares a birth chart, or horoscope, for an individual, it is a two-dimensional record of these three-dimensional events in the heavens, represented graphically as a wheel encompassing concentric rings. The Earth is the pinpoint at the centre of the wheel and is surrounded by twelve fixed segments representing the zodiacal Houses, the areas of life in which planetary influences will manifest themselves. The outer circle of the chart represents the moving zodiacal corridor, divided into its twelve segments – the signs of the zodiac.

The predictability of the planets' movements has enabled astrologers to create tables, known as Ephemerides, of the planetary positions past, present and future. Once the positions of the Sun, Moon and planets have been established for a specific time, and a particular subject, the astrologer can assess and interpret what effects the planets will have, how they will enhance, diminish or frustrate each other's powers, and which areas of the subject's life will come under their particular influences. And all of this information is blended with the astrologer's understanding of the sun sign personality, the broad framework of individuality in zodiacal terms.

THE GEMINI PERSONALITY

 emini is the third sign of the zodiac. Clever, charming and curious, shrewd, versatile and adaptable, active, alert and agile, Gemini craves change, distractions, new experiences and sensations. The Geminian ideal is to sample everything and talk to everyone. Reading a book, watching television and holding a three-way conversation all at the same time is standard Gemini behaviour. Geminis adore talk, debate, discussion and can leap from side to side in an argument with all the ease of the daring young man on the flying trapeze, elaborating a little learning into a dazzling thing. Gemini is the zodiac's jack-of-all-trades, the snapper-up of unconsidered trifles; but it can also be jack-the-lad, as a Gemini without sufficient variety in life and work may well be seduced by the company of villains. Gemini's ability to keep so many balls and plates in the air at the same time can make the rest of the zodiac feel tired.

Relaxing and doing nothing are well nigh impossible for restless Geminians. They adore being hurried from sport to sport: too unreliable for team games and too impatient for the dull slog of training, they go for the badminton court, the dance class, the archery range. For Gemini is the butterfly of the zodiac, and butterflies should not be broken on the wheel of routine. If the shadow of predictability looms over his or her bright, ever-changing world, Gemini may well run away with the gypsies or leave town with the circus.

Gemini
Orbis Regens
Mercurius Ⅱ
Signum Obstans
Sagittarius ♐

THE PLANETARY RULER

ncient astrologers named the five planets they could see in the night sky after the five most powerful classical gods; naturally, the planets took on the attributes and associations of the gods, and a pleasingly symmetrical system was devised to distribute this planetary power throughout the zodiac.

The Sun and Moon, being the most dazzling lights, ruled one sun sign each (Leo and Cancer). The remaining ten signs managed under the shared patronage of the five planets. Mercury presided over Gemini and Virgo, Venus over Taurus and Libra, Mars over Aries and Scorpio, Jupiter over Sagittarius and Pisces, and Saturn over Aquarius and Capricorn.

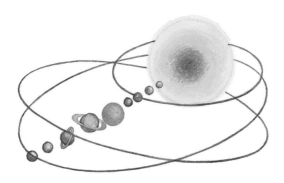

When more planets were discovered after the invention of the telescope in 1610, a reshuffle became necessary. Uranus (discovered in 1781) was allocated to Aquarius, Neptune (1836) was thought appropriate for Pisces, and Pluto (1930) now broods over Scorpio. This has unbalanced the symmetry: the search is on for other planets to share the burden with Venus and Mercury. Indeed, the asteroid Chiron, discovered in 1977 looping

the void between Saturn and Uranus, is considered by some astrologers to be the suitable governor of Virgo.

The planetary power behind Gemini comes from Mercury, the messenger of the gods. Mercury represents communication and intelligence, intellectual and reasoning power, quick-thinking and resourcefulness, comprehension and expression, verbal skills and cerebral fancy. It is versatile, lively, playful and curious. Adversely, the influence of Mercury can produce chronic restlessness, inconsistency, nervousness, inquisitiveness and an addiction to low cunning.

Astronomically, Mercury is the innermost planet of the Solar System. Dense and small (it could almost be lost in the Atlantic Ocean), it dashes around the Sun once every eighty-eight days, and may stay a few days or a few weeks in each zodiac sign. It is so close to the Sun that its vigorous twinkle is often outshone – it can occasionally be seen low in the east at sunrise and low in the west at dusk. The Greeks named it after Hermes, the messenger of their gods: Mercury is the Roman name for Hermes.

GEMINI

PATTERNS IN THE STARS

tar pictures, or images of the constellations, are formed in the eye of the beholder. What we see as a neighbourly cluster is usually an optical illusion, the stars in the group being many light years apart. Even so, the urge to impose a friendly pattern on the frosty immensity of the night sky, to link the stars with the myths and legends on earth has been irresistible to all cultures. Different cultures make out different pictures, and the results are sometimes inscrutable – searching for Leo, say, you will look in vain for the shape of a lion pricked out in stars against the dark backcloth of the night sky.

The zodiac constellations were among the first to be made out, as they were the star groups that formed the background to the moving planets, providing a useful reference grid to plot planetary movements. These gave their names to the signs of the zodiac, although they spread unevenly across the sky and are not tidily confined to the equal 30-degree segments of the imaginary zodiac band. Many stars are known by their Arabic names, and the star that shone brightest in each constellation when Arabic astrologers first compiled their star catalogues was designated its alpha.

The constellation that gave its name to the third sign of the zodiac is the northern star group Gemini the Twins, a glittering swirl crossed by the galactic splendour of the Milky Way. Huge and spectacular, Gemini contains the impressive star cluster prosaically known as M35, which is visible to the naked eye, as well as eleven very bright stars. Castor and Pollux are the most important: historically Castor, the alpha, was the brightest star, but today Pollux shines brighter.

Gemini is the starry image of the inseparable twin heroes Castor and Pollux (known as Polydeuces to the Romans). Outstanding athletes, warriors and poets, they were the brothers of the original *femme fatale*, Helen of Troy, and the sons of the immortal and prolific Zeus by the mortal Leda, Queen of Sparta. Castor was mortal, Pollux immortal. After many adventures and heroic quests, Castor finally fell, fatally wounded in battle. The grief-stricken Pollux begged to die with him, but Zeus refused this request, instead placing the brothers to shine together forever among the stars.

THE ATTRACTION OF OPPOSITES

n astrological terms, polarity describes the strong complementary relationship between signs that are exactly opposite each other on the zodiac circle, 180 degrees or six signs apart. These signs share the same gender – masculine or feminine – and the same quality – cardinal, fixed or mutable – and so share the ways they look at the world and shape their energy. Characteristics and interests complement each other or harmonize on different scales.

Relationships between polar signs are often very satisfying and fruitful, especially in the context of work. A clue to this affinity lies with the elements governed by each sign. The mathematics of polarity mean that earth signs oppose only water signs, and that fire opposes only air. Fire and air signs therefore encourage and inspire each other – fire cannot burn without air and air needs heat to rise. Earth and water signs conspire together creatively – earth without water is unfruitful, water unconfined by earth wastes

its energy in diffusion – and together they make mud, rich material for any creative process.

Six signs away from bright, sprightly Gemini, the bantering butterfly whose twin ambitions are to try everything once and talk to everybody on the planet, we find Sagittarius the Centaur, the deep-chested hunter. Just as addicted to challenge, diversity and exploration but with more stamina, application, penetration and insight, Sagittarius is the seeker of truth and wisdom rather than facts and information.

More than in any of the other five polarity pairings in the zodiac, the affinity between Gemini and Sagittarius is self-evident; the difference is a matter of degree. In both signs, a shared and complementary shaping energy is at work, the mutable energy of transformation. Both Gemini and Sagittarius preside over times of the year that are the spaces between the dissolution of the old season and the evolution of the new, when all is exhilaratingly potential and everything is tantalizingly open to exploration.

The complementary aspect of polarity is also seen in the characteristics traditionally associated with the two signs. Both are restless seekers after knowledge, both highly mobile, both anxious to patrol the frontiers and report back.

Gemini, the air sign, spreads to cover as much surface as possible; Sagittarius, the fire sign, has a flickering versatility and intellectual power that can illuminate the dark.

THE SYMBOLS OF THE ZODIAC

ver since astrology began, there has been a kind of astrological shorthand, a set of symbols or ideograms called glyphs. Glyphs make the language of astrology universal and available to people who have no literary tradition. They also make it easy to draw up a birthchart, a convenient form of notation, especially when planets are clustered in one area of the chart.

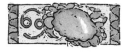

Each of the zodiac signs has its own glyph, as do the planets. They have evolved over centuries, and so are now freighted with symbolism, not simply convenient codes.

Today, the glyph for Gemini is a simple representation of the Roman numeral II, joined at top and bottom by slightly curved lines. Early Egyptians were more explicit, the Gemini hieroglyph being recognizably two small male figures holding hands, brother 'pin-men'. The Greeks had two

symbols, one an ornate H, with the two uprights joined by a down-curving line, the other a hastily scrawled G. Medieval astrologers had two versions, one being two undulating parallel horizontal lines, the other a prototype of the modern glyph.

There is a special fascination in studying the glyphs to see what other symbolism may be contained within them. The Gemini glyph represents conjoined dualism, the doubleness that is an essential prerequisite to life: masculine and feminine, conscious and unconscious, yin and yang. Interchange and progress can happen only when there are two principles involved.

Planets also have their glyphs, and the Mercury symbol is rather complex, evoking once more the dualism that characterizes both Gemini and its ruling planet. The glyph is a circle mounted on a cross (like that for Venus), but surmounting the circle is an upward-curving semicircle, which is reminiscent both of Mercury's winged helmet and the horns that typically symbolize maleness.

THE HOUSE OF GEMINI

he twelve Houses are an intellectual concept, not a physical reality, an expression of all the aspects of human life and experience, from the self to the infinite. Each is associated with a sign of the zodiac, sharing its planetary ruler and elemental energy. However, the Houses are fixed and constant – they are represented by the

central numbered segments on a birth chart – and the signs and planets pass through them. They are the channels through which planetary and zodiacal energies flow and indicate which area of life is the focus of particular zodiacal influence at any one time.

Gemini, being the third sign of the zodiac, rules the Third House, which is also overseen by Gemini's planetary ruler, Mercury. Like Gemini, the Third House is permeated by air energy, and therefore concerns itself with mental and intellectual activity, and all levels of communication and social interaction. In particular, the Third House is concerned with the expansion and expression of ourselves in the world, with family ties – especially siblings – and with education, communication,

correspondence, transport and commerce, the first steps out into the world beyond the solid base of the Second House.

As Mercury governs this House, it is also concerned with the life of the mind, the gathering, interpretation and exchange of experience and information. The planet (or planets if any), in the Third House at the time of birth influence the ways in which people express themselves and deal with their relationships and with their environment.

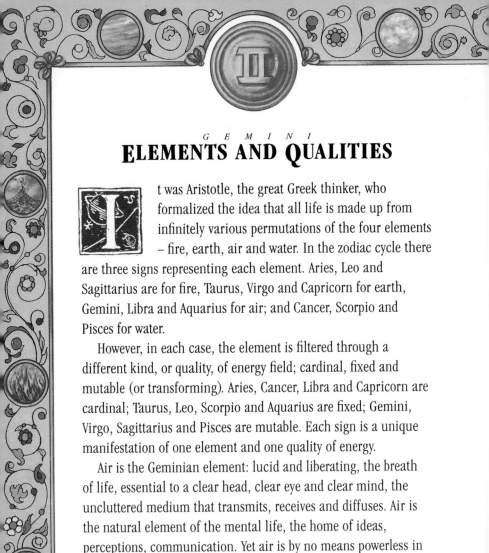

ELEMENTS AND QUALITIES

I t was Aristotle, the great Greek thinker, who formalized the idea that all life is made up from infinitely various permutations of the four elements – fire, earth, air and water. In the zodiac cycle there are three signs representing each element. Aries, Leo and Sagittarius are for fire, Taurus, Virgo and Capricorn for earth, Gemini, Libra and Aquarius for air; and Cancer, Scorpio and Pisces for water.

However, in each case, the element is filtered through a different kind, or quality, of energy field; cardinal, fixed and mutable (or transforming). Aries, Cancer, Libra and Capricorn are cardinal; Taurus, Leo, Scorpio and Aquarius are fixed; Gemini, Virgo, Sagittarius and Pisces are mutable. Each sign is a unique manifestation of one element and one quality of energy.

Air is the Geminian element: lucid and liberating, the breath of life, essential to a clear head, clear eye and clear mind, the uncluttered medium that transmits, receives and diffuses. Air is the natural element of the mental life, the home of ideas, perceptions, communication. Yet air is by no means powerless in the material world. This is the element that can gently fan your overheated brow or savagely rip the roof off your home, bring rainclouds to refresh parched crops or work itself up into a hurricane that devastates whole cities.

Gemini yearns to be as free as air, flitting from project to project, place to place, as quickly as possible. Speeding through

the air like wing-heeled Mercury is the Geminian dream; and a Gemini piloting a hang-glider is, in all senses, in heaven.

Geminian energy is mutable. Mutable energy people change the rules; they are the movers, transformers, changers, confidently releasing the potential of their particular energy. Gemini's air energy is a light yet insistent breeze, rustling the leaves of experience, broadcasting the seeds of ideas, dancing from tree to flower, hill to dale. For Gemini, the answers are always blowing in the wind.

THE ZODIAC GARDEN

otoring along in an open-top roadster, pistoning along on a twenty-gear all-terrain bike, or simply loping along a country lane, Gemini loves to be on the move, through pleasantly changing rural vistas. Woodlands enchant Geminians, fragrant glades spangled with jewel-bright flowers like a page from a medieval book of hours.

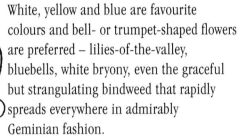

White, yellow and blue are favourite colours and bell- or trumpet-shaped flowers are preferred – lilies-of-the-valley, bluebells, white bryony, even the graceful but strangulating bindweed that rapidly spreads everywhere in admirably Geminian fashion.

The Geminian appreciation of the garden is intellectual; Geminis love being in it, but would rather it sprang fully formed into the world from the mind of the goddess Flora than that it should involve a great deal of tedious, patient work. The ideal Geminian garden will have a bright greensward, a gnarled old walnut tree and energetic, adventurous flowering plants – creepers, trailers and climbers such as wisteria, honeysuckle, clematis and rambling white roses. Scent is very important, emanating from wallflowers, stocks and sweet peas. If there is a kitchen garden, it will have herbs and vegetables that are ornamental and fragrant, to beguile the eye and nose as well as the palate – lavender and lemon balm, white-flowered caraway and aniseed, bushy marjoram and stout myrtle shrubs, and carrots which produce bright frondy tops.

Gemini likes to keep house and garden separate, to promote stimulating differences in daily surroundings. The Geminian interior will not be a florist's dream, although cut flowers are favoured, especially white ones: sweet-smelling freesias, for example, arranged with plenty of filmy, ferny greenery. Pot-plants are altogether too much of a responsibility, but a white azalea might become a cherished possession.

I had a little nut tree,
Nothing would it bear
But a silver nutmeg
And a golden pear.
The king of Spain's daughter
Came to visit me,
All for the sake of my little nut tree.

Traditional English Poem

ASTROLOGY AND THE ARK

he word zodiac comes from the Greek word for living creatures, and many of the signs are symbolized by animals. Gemini, however, is among the minority represented by human figures. In this case, the image is of the heavenly heroic twins, Castor and Pollux, perfect for a sign whose natives are quite capable of doing two different things at the same time and who are nearly always in two minds about most things.

Even so, there are animals associated with Gemini; charming, delightful, attractive animals who symbolize the sign's characteristics: monkeys, for instance, insatiably curious, brilliant mimics, funny, endearing and very naughty, their clever little hands capable of delicate manipulation; butterflies, flitting from blossom to bloom, never stopping to rest or recollect, cramming their short gaudy lives with experience; little birds, ceaselessly twittering and fluttering, seeming to live on a faster timescale than the rest of us; and parrots, living wild in great raucous rainbow flocks, non-stop communicators who even mimic the languages of other species.

Gemini's ruler, Mercury, is almost overwhelmed with responsibilities as a god. One of them is the care of animals in general, specifically the herds and flocks that represented the triumph of human resourcefulness over the raw material of nature. It was the domestication of the animals that made it possible for people to settle permanently in one place rather than travel behind their animal food sources, a great socializing force in early civilizations.

Restless Geminis, ever ready to jet off in all directions, are not the best pet owners; they will only remember the unfed cat when stuck on a delayed flight circling over Kennedy airport. All Geminis love a flutter, and are likely to be seen in the stands at racecourses. Some may even be riding the horses; Gemini jockeys are quick-thinking, intuitive, responsive and resourceful – and they adore wearing the bright silks.

GEMINI ON THE MAP

undane astrology charts the birth of nations: countries, cities and major towns come under zodiacal influence, just as their inhabitants do. Often the ascendant, the sign in the First House which characterizes the nation as a whole, is more significant than the sun sign. Various methods are used to assess which zodiac sign holds sway where. Countries with an incontestable birthday – Christmas Day 1066, the day William the Conqueror was crowned king of England, for instance – have a standard birth chart. In countries which have evolved more organically, zodiacal influences may be deduced by the broad characteristics – can you think of a more suitable ruling sign than Taurus for Switzerland, the land loud with cowbells? Cities and towns may show their zodiacal allegiance by their function – most spas are ruled by health-conscious Virgo, and the administrative heart of any capital city is ruled by Capricorn, the zodiac's bureaucrat.

Gemini's worldly subjects include the United States of America, Wales and Belgium. There could not be a country more Geminian than the USA, founded on the notion of the brotherhood of man, always the first at the frontiers of knowledge and experience, gregarious, noisy, constantly communicating – by phone, fax, modem, radio, video, newspaper, train, plane and road. Wales mass-produces (and exports) Geminian archetypes in bulk: teachers, talkers, sportsmen, doctors, poets and bards. Belgium, of course, is the centre of the European Economic Community, and is a country almost entirely dedicated to the spirit of the marketplace – Gemini's ruler Mercury is the merchant's god. Other Geminian countries include Armenia, Sardinia and Lower Egypt.

Cities under Gemini include the city that never sleeps – New York, New York (so good they named it twice); London, a mass of markets linked by a river of commerce; Bruges, the monument to medieval merchants; Nuremburg (Nürnberg) home of hierarchic trades guilds and intricate, fascinating toys; San Francisco, queen of America's west coast, dedicated to interpersonal experiences. Other Geminian towns are Cardiff, Plymouth, Melbourne, Metz, Cordoba and Versailles.

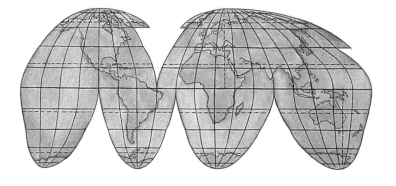

EARTH'S BOUNTY

ood plants associated with Gemini are carrots, leafy vegetables (apart from cabbage) and nuts of all kinds, especially hazel and walnuts; all quick and easy to prepare, they can even be eaten raw if Gemini is really in a rush. To this sign belong light, pretty foods packed with nutrition – just the diet to encourage a lively mind; no post-prandial "armchairobics" for Gemini.

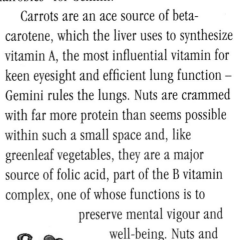

Carrots are an ace source of beta-carotene, which the liver uses to synthesize vitamin A, the most influential vitamin for keen eyesight and efficient lung function – Gemini rules the lungs. Nuts are crammed with far more protein than seems possible within such a small space and, like greenleaf vegetables, they are a major source of folic acid, part of the B vitamin complex, one of whose functions is to preserve mental vigour and well-being. Nuts and carrots both offer the doubleness Gemini loves: sweet carrot cake or spicy carrot soup; salted peanuts or sugared almonds.

Dining with Gemini will always be an adventure; the kitchen is not the hub of the home, but it will bristle with the very latest culinary gadgets – whizzers, blenders, shredders, juicers, mixers, microwaves, herb-grinders, designer kettles; and there will be the most exotic spice rack you've ever seen, full of colours and flavours from faraway places.

Expect to eat the latest cuisine and drink excellent light and fruity wine from California and the New World.

Geminis really prefer to dine out – at power lunches or gossipy dinners where they can eat and talk at the same time. Find them in modish brasseries, where the chattering classes browse, or at the smartest and newest place to eat – Gemini will be the first to sniff out the latest Lithuanian or Javanese café on the block. Food that offers maximum variety with an exotic topspin seduces the Geminian palate – Indonesian *rijsttafel*, Greek *meze*, Japanese *sushi*. And, of course, fast food and Gemini were made for each other, although fast does not equal junk: the sandwich, slapped together by the rakish Earl of Sandwich who was too busy to leave the gaming tables, is pure Gemini.

A HEAVENLY HERBAL

erbs and the heavens have been linked forever; for many centuries, herbs were the only medicine, and the gathering and application of them were guided by the planets. Doctors would learn the rudiments of astrology as a matter of course – Hippocrates claimed that 'a physician without a knowledge of astrology had no right to call himself a physician'.

Healing plants and their ruling planets were often linked via the elements – fire, water, air and earth. Mars, for example, a hot fiery planet, self-evidently rules over hot, fiery plants such as mustard. Herbs that cure the ills of particular parts of the body are ruled by the planet that governs that part of the body. Plants are also assigned according to what they look like. For example, walnuts, which look like tiny models of the brain, are ruled by Mercury, the planet which rules the brain.

All herbs are more effective if they are gathered on a day ruled by their patron planet, especially at dawn, when they are fat with sap drawn up by the beams of the Moon, or at dusk, after a day basking in the strengthening rays of the Sun.

Gemini rules aniseed, caraway and marjoram, all versatile plants that contribute to time-honoured folk remedies for mind and body, as well as to delicious sweet and savoury dishes and pungent, powerful liqueurs. Strong-tasting aniseed is an ancient cure for hiccups and flatulence, and is used by the modern pharmaceutical industry to make cough medicines and pastilles.

According to Pliny, chewing sugar-dredged aniseed keeps the breath sweet (great for non-stop talkers), and Pythagoras theorized that a handful of aniseed stalks under the pillow can chase away bad dreams.

Caraway offers another cure for colic and wind, and contains lots of phosphorous, excellent fuel for the brain. Nicolas Culpeper's original herbal provides a recipe for little caraway sweets to cure colds, bronchial troubles and wind. Marjoram is best known as one quarter of the cook's staple, *bouquet garni*; but marjoram oil in a warm bath or as a massage soothes and strengthens fretful Gemini nerves. A decoction of the leaves makes an excellent gargle and clears the head and sinuses of a heavy cold. Marjoram is also reputed to drive away witches and diabolic spirits, real or imagined.

THE CELESTIAL BODY

ach part of the body comes under the influence of a
different zodiac sign. Appropriately for a double
sign, Gemini rules the shoulders and arms. Active,
bustling Gemini, often with more irons in the fire
than can be practically handled, frequently complains of a
sprained or broken hand, wrist, arm or shoulder, of tennis elbow,
or the repeated stress syndrome induced by crouching too long
over the word processor, intent on beating a deadline.

As the part of the body ruled by the polar sign often causes
health problems, Geminis might also suffer
from similar aches and sprains
in the hips and

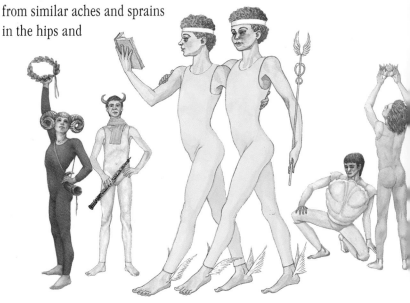

thighs, which come under Sagittarius's patronage. Gemini itself also rules the nerves, and as friends of Geminians will attest, they often have a very short fuse and get rid of a lot of nervous energy by flying off the handle and leaping to conclusions.

The planets are thought to govern body systems, and Gemini's ruler, Mercury, is associated with the lungs and respiratory system and the brain and nervous system, both concerned with interface and exchange, linking and connecting us with the world.

Geminis are very prone to colds, which may develop into bronchitis. Plenty of lettuce and cauliflower in the diet help combat this tendency. After a hard day running the world, Geminis should try to relax in a warm bath laced with therapeutic oils: marjoram, lavender, basil, sandalwood, pine, bergamot and juniper soothe respiratory problems and float away anxieties.

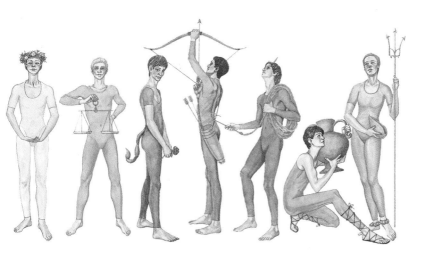

THE STARS AND THE STONES

 unes are a code, secret keys to the different facets of the whole interconnecting universe. Originated by the Germanic nomads who wandered the plains of northern Italy some 500 years before Christ, this compact and portable form of magic crossed the Alps and spread throughout northern Europe and Scandinavia. The twenty-four 'letters' of the *futharc* (an acronym of the first six letters of the runic alphabet) were used by the pragmatic Germans as a straightforward recording medium, as well as a shortcut to tapping the secrets of the universe. Each rune is a powerpacked symbol of one aspect of existence – for example, the fourth rune *As* means ash tree, but also signifies the tree of the world, the divine force that controls the cosmic order.

When the runes are cast, they combine, and the trained runemaster can read what has been, what is, and what influences are shaping future events. Authentic ancient runes, the portable arkana, were carved or painted on fresh-cut fruitwood and cast onto a white cloth for divination, but pebble or stone runes work just as well. Everyone should make their own runes – they have personal power, and they are free.

Runic astrology divides the sky into twenty-four segments, or seles, which correspond with the futharc. The seles modify the expression of the planetary energy as each planet passes through them. The planets carry the attributes of the northern gods, and these too have runic associations.

As the sun signs do not coincide with the runic seles, they often come under the influence of two or more runes. The Gemini runes are *Ing, Odal* and *Dag. Ing*, a beacon, beams its message of reason and intelligence through the dark night; *Odal*, meaning homeland, represents community, native intelligence and resourcefulness, inherited folk wisdom. *Dag*, day, the last letter of the futharc, is the rune of midsummer, signifying clarity, openness, the clear light of reason. The runic image of Gemini as compulsive communicator, sparkling intellect and dedicated social being, intent on gathering and sharing knowledge, be it profound or trivial, is remarkably similar to the zodiacal profile.

Along with *Odal*, *As* and *Gyfu* are the runes associated with Gemini's ruler Mercury, whose northern equivalent is Odin, the god of wisdom who snatched the secret of the runes from the world tree Yggdrasil. *As*, the ash tree, also means god, specifically Odin; and *Gyfu*, meaning gift or talent, embraces the Geminian imperative of sharing and interchange.

These be the book runes
And the runes of good help
And all the taboo runes
And the runes of much might.

from *The Edda*

39

ZODIAC TREASURE

he zodiac treasure hoard may overflow with gorgeous gems, but it is guarded by grumpy and confused dragons, who squabble among themselves and cannot agree on which stone best fits which sign. However, the beguiling idea of a jewelled girdle encircling the zodiac is an ancient one, and may even be based on the twelve gemstones, one for each of the tribes of Israel, set on the breastplate of the Jewish high-priests of biblical times. Medieval astrologers felt reasonably sure of their ground and listed the gems as follows, in zodiacal order: bloodstone, sapphire, agate, emerald,

onyx, carnelian, chrysolite, aquamarine, topaz, ruby, garnet and amethyst. Catherine de Medici, the original power-dresser, was rumoured to possess a glittering belt of zodiacal gems.

As there is no real consensus in the matter, a new approach is needed. Consideration of the colour and characteristics traditionally attributed to each sun sign may lead to a satisfying match of sign with stone.

Gemini's colour is yellow – bright yellow, chrome yellow, enamel yellow – although it will be in the nature of Gemini to argue strenuously for a whole rainbow of other colours as well. In effect this means that Geminis can wear any gemstone they like – and they do –

but there are two (of course) specifically associated with this sign, agate and chrysoprase.

Agate is self-evidently Geminian: not only does it come in enough varieties to vault over Gemini's ground-level boredom threshold, but within each individual stone different colours layer and swirl, effectively avoiding any tedious repetition. White and amber agate, a blend of white (itself the sum of all colours) and of Gemini's own colour, yellow, perhaps best reflects the sign's inherent duality. Moss agate, a soothing blend of olive and leaf colours, will calm restless twin souls. Chrysoprase, a light, bright quartz the colour of young leek shoots will attract the Geminian eye for the unusual.

Look for modern pieces when jewellery shopping for Gemini – lightweight, clear-coloured materials such as aluminium, plastic or enamel, and unusual design. Best of all, commission something special from an avant-garde design studio before it becomes a household name – Gemini loves to be ahead of the game.

EARTH'S HIDDEN POWER

Beneath the earth, in the realm of Pluto, lie the solidified energies, metals and crystals that hum with compacted potency.

Gemini's metal is mercury, otherwise known as quicksilver, the disconcertingly mobile silver-white metal that is never still, moving and flowing incessantly, scattering into heavy little globules and recoagulating before your very eyes. Mercury responds so quickly to its environment that it can accurately measure minute changes in temperature. It is also extremely poisonous. Consequently it is difficult, not to say downright dangerous, for Geminians to fill their homes with their native metal. Expect to see lots of hi-tech chrome, mirrored-glass furniture and whizzy designer gadgets and games instead. Wealthier Geminis are fond of platinum, and will wear it as jewellery or impressive wristwatches.

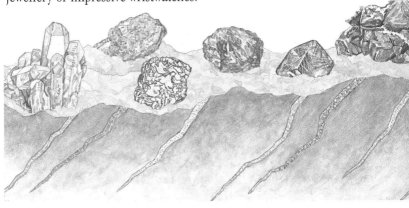

Crystals are chemical elements compressed over millenia into dense, solid form, storehouses of electromagnetic energy. Gemini, naturally, has two powerful crystals, agate and chrysoprase; and as Geminian objects are decorative and useful at the same time, these crystals are beautiful enough to be worn as gemstones. Agate, a variety of chalcedony, strengthens the connection between mind and body, calms jumpy Geminian nerves, and promotes strength of mind to temper mercurial mood swings. Chrysoprase, a gorgeous green variety of quartz, combats neurotic imbalance, enhances intuitive powers, promotes optimism and *joie de vivre* and encourages the spirit of successful enterprise. As long ago as the fourth century BC, Alexander the Great wore an amulet of chrysoprase to help him conquer and rule the ancient world.

Gemini's ruling planet, Mercury, also opts for agate, specifically the dual crystal, the white and amber agate which Geminis like to wear as jewellery. The intermingled stripes mix the soothing, strengthening qualities of cool white agate with the properties of warm yellow amber, which activates the intellect.

GEMINI ON THE CARDS

ometimes called the Devil's Picture Book, the tarot was probably created in the twelfth century, but its origins are suitably shrouded in secrecy. There are seventy-eight cards: twenty-two in the Major Arcana, a gallery of enigmatic archetypal images from the Fool via the Wheel of Fortune to the World, and fifty-six in the Minor Arcana, divided into four suits – coins, cups, swords and batons (or wands).

Tarot cards, being one of the ways to explore the human psyche, have an affinity with the zodiac sun signs, and cards from the Major Arcana and the court cards from the Minor Arcana are associated with specific signs and their ruling planets.

Traditionally, Gemini has no card in the Major Arcana, but is represented in the Minor Arcana by the Knight of Batons, or Wands. This carefree young man rides on a dashing white charger (Castor,

the mortal Gemini, was a famous horse-tamer). He is unarmed, open, alert, inventive, intuitive, intelligent – confidently holding out his baton, intent on relaying ideas and information. When crossed, however, he can be evasive, argumentative, a fomentor of baseless discord, and economical with the truth.

Gemini's ruler Mercury is associated with the Magician, a very powerful, complex figure, the second card in the Major Arcana, but assigned the number one as the Fool, the first card, has no number. The Magician controls the whole of the Minor Arcana. His stage props are miniature cups, balls, sticks and a small sword, and his distinctive hat, shaped like a lateral figure of eight, symbolizes his allegiance to Hermes (Mercury), whose sacred occult number is eight. The Magician is intelligent, versatile, flexible, clever, dextrous and manipulative; like the travelling player which represents him on the cards, he is always on the move, quick to use his skill and intellect to transform the realities of the world around him, fascinated by the many possible paths to wisdom. The downside of the Magician is the juggler, the smart tricksy deceiver, using his manipulative powers to bedazzle the slower witted.

There are many ways to lay out the tarot cards for a reading, but a particularly zodiacal one is to place the significator (the card chosen to represent the questioner) in the centre and lay out the other cards in a circle anticlockwise, starting from the nine o'clock position. This follows the layout of the astrological Houses, and the cards are interpreted in the context of the House in which they fall.

INDEX